EXCURSIONS
into
FYLDE HISTORY

David Foster

Published by Hendon Publishing Co., Ltd., Hendon Mill, Nelson, Lancs.
Text and maps © David Foster.
Printed by Turner & Earnshaw Ltd., Westway House, Sycamore Avenue, Burnley, Lancs.

Introduction

During the last twenty years the study of the landscapes of the past has become a subject worthy of serious attention, thanks largely to Professor W.G. Hoskins whose research has reached a wide audience through the publication of his pioneering work *The Making of the English Landscape* by Penguin Books in 1955 and by the various television programmes which he has made on the same theme. A further filip to the increasing interest in the evidence of previous environments was provided by the celebration of European Architectural Heritage Year in 1975. Government funds were made available for renovation schemes such as the cleaning of churches and public buildings, and town, villages and individuals produced a variety of local guides; in consequence we were all made more aware of the potential and the richness of our local environments.

Some landscapes, such as the mediaeval towns of Chester and York, the military fortresses of North Wales or the gaunt factory towns of the Pennines, are obvious areas of interest to both the professional and the tourist; others are apparently less rewarding in that they have no immediately apparent features which recall previous societies, and the Fylde is such a region. It is not blessed with any outstanding cathedrals or parish churches, it does not possess major examples of polite or vernacular architecture of any period, its military remains are non-existent and its industrial archaelogy is limited. From the sixteenth century onwards, Britain was regularly recorded by keen topographers — John Leland, Camden and Daniel Defoe, to name but a handful of the most famous — but the majority either ignored the Fylde or accorded it scant mention in their works. The explanation of this lack of attraction to the traveller is to be found in the region's isolation from the main arteries of national life, perhaps the dominant factor in its history until the advent of the large-scale holiday industry on the coast in the second half of the nineteenth century. The relative poverty which this remoteness incurred has ensured the absence of major architectural monuments of previous generations, and its lack of facilities for industrial development helped to maintain its traditional character.

Despite this unpromising picture, the Fylde is far more than the apparently flat, even monotonous area through which people rush by railway or motorway to the entertainments of the coast. Between the Bowland fells to the east and the urban spread on the west coast there lies a region of small market towns and quiet villages with a history of continuous settlement from Roman times and possibly much earlier. Implicit in this book is the idea that every contemporary landscape is a product of man's struggle with his environment throughout human history and a record of his achievements and his failures. The villages and their houses, the farms in their fields, the roads and the railways, the churches and the chapels all speak to us of the past, and to those who pause long enough to look the clues to the Fylde's history can be read in the landscape. However, no historian would argue that the development of human society can be fully understood in terms of artefacts and landscapes. The clues in the landscape will only yield up their solutions when read in conjunction with the wide range of documentary evidence which is available for most regions. Therefore this book has two elements. One invites the interested traveller to enjoy the Fylde landscape by undertaking walks and excursions; the other attempts to explain the visual in terms of the historical developments of the societies and communities which have lived there.

Many people have contributed to the production of this book, including many of my former students, but I am particularly grateful to Mr. P. Schofield of Thornton-Cleveleys who provided the photography and to my colleague Mr. H.L. Phillips for cartographical advice. My friend and former colleague Mr. A.R. Wilson will recognise his influence on the work at many points.

David Foster.

Table of Contents

	Page
Introduction	3
Fylde Villages	5
Garstang	17
Kirkham and Wesham	23
Poulton-le-Fylde	29

Map references in the text are all on O.S. Sheet 102, 1:50,000 First Series.

Fylde Villages

The majority of Fylde villages can be found in one of two kinds of site — on the small hillocks which abound in the region, and close to water be it river or sea. When the last ice-sheet receded from the area c. 10–15,000 years ago, it left large deposits of boulder clay and glacial outwash material all over the Fylde, and many of those sites have been colonised by man in subsequent times simply because they were dry-points in a wilderness of marsh and fen and because their superior drainage rendered them more suitable for cultivation, an important factor in a subsistence economy. A vital adjunct to farming, both arable and pastoral, in those far-off days was fishing, both in streams and in-shore, and it is inevitable that some early settlements in the Fylde would be planted around the coast, both of the Irish Sea and Morecambe Bay, and along the rivers Wyre and Ribble. With these villages, the same need for a dry-point site was present, and they are to be found some distance from the alluvial flats of the rivers, such as Great Eccleston on the river Wyre and Freckleton on the Ribble estuary.

One of the most casual and ordinary, yet important and difficult questions about settlements relates to their antiquity. It is impossible to be precise about the origins and dating of villages, hamlets and farms, particularly in the north of England where life appears to have been more precarious than in the south, though some authorities believe that in most parts of the British Isles there has been uninterrupted occupation of many sites since pre-Roman times. As far as one can tell, there is no reliable documentary evidence before the Domesday Book (1086) nor any significant archaeological material which might illuminate the early settlement patterns of the Fylde. The 'Blackpool Elk', a prehistoric find of the late 1960s, indicates some primitive habitation of the region, and local antiquaries have long been convinced of a substantial Roman presence in the Fylde, though to date the firm evidence points only to a small fort at Kirkham and a road from Ribchester which has been traced to a point two miles west of the fort (102/ 396337). Whether there was a Roman port (the mysterious Portus Setantiorum) at the mouth of the river Wyre and whether the road ran further west to serve it is only speculative at present.

However, the study of placenames supplies a considerable amount of information about the early settlement pattern of the Fylde and points to the continuity of occupation since pre-Roman times and to a remarkably varied racial history. The evidence reveals three main stages of settlement:

1. Celtic. One of the greatest placename authorities, Professor Eckwall, has drawn attention to the remarkable number of villages and hamlets in the Fylde with wholly- or partially-British (i.e. pre-Roman) placename elements. Examples are Great and Little Eccleston (the Welsh *eglwys* leading to *eccles* or church); Preese in Weeton-with-Preese and Presall (the Welsh *prys* or *pes* meaning brushwood). The rivers tell a similar story. Wyre, Cocker, Savick Brook and Pilling all come from British names.

2. Anglian. The Anglian settlement of Lancashire began in the late sixth century A.D. and came from the east; although it continued for several centuries, the main lines had been drawn by the mid-seventh century. There are three principal stages: (i) c.570 A.D., indicated by the *–ing* settlements such as Staining and Bryning; (ii) c.600 A.D., the *–ham* settlements as in Bispham and Lytham; (iii) after 615 A.D., the *–tun* settlements such as Clifton, Hambleton, Marton, Thornton and Weeton. The Anglian newcomers were chiefly farmers from the Low Countries of northern Europe and they naturally sought the more fertile spots in which to create permanent homes. In the Fylde, this meant the boulder clay hummocks and other glacial deposits prominent in the centre of the region, a point emphasised by the general absence of Anglian placenames in the marshy areas of the south-west and to the north of the river Wyre.

3. Norse. The Norse settlement of the Fylde took place from c.900 A.D., rather later than in the south and east of the country, and was carried out by Norsemen who had emigrated to Ireland and the Isle of Man before crossing the Irish sea up to a century later. Thus, it is more accurate to speak of an Irish-Norse and Manx-Norse than a pure Norse settlement of the Fylde. These largely pastoral folk have left their mark in such placename elements as *—by* (a village) in Ribby, Sowerby and Westby; *—breck* (a slope) as in Larbreck, Norbreck and Warbreck; *—scaela* (a hut) in Scales; and *—argh* or *—ergh* as in Medlar and Kellermargh, an interesting reference to the Scandanavian practice of summer pasturing their cattle away from the main homestead. In contrast to the popular picture of bloodthirsty invaders who plundered the communities which they found, the Norsemen who came to the Fylde may well have been fairly peaceful folk who settled cheek-by-jowl with their Anglian predecessors. This interpretation is suggested by the large number of townships which have composite names, one element Anglian the other Norse, as in Bispham-with-Norbreck, Layton-with-Warbreck and Newton-with -Scales. Most remarkable of all is the township of Treales, Roseacre and Wharles which contains one British element (*Treulas*, the village with a court), one Anglian *(hwerfel*, a circle and *hlaw*, a mound) and one Norse (*Raysacre*, the field with a cairn). However, one wonders whether the Scandanavian modification of earlier Anglian names indicates that the Norse settlement of the Fylde was not entirely peaceful; this can be seen in Carleton, Kirkham, Rawcliffe and Staynall. Nontheless, the predominant impression is one of parallel colonisation with the Norse newcomers filling in the less attractive areas which the Anglians had avoided, thus leading to an expansion of settlement into the north and the south-west of the region.

It will not have escaped the careful reader that some of the placenames mentioned above also imply the existence of some pre-Norman churches in the Fylde, perhaps at Bispham, Great Eccleston and Kirkham. Furthermore, the dedication of present-day churches to Anglian saints at Poulton-le-Fylde (St. Chad) and Lytham (St. Cuthbert) might also point to the possibility of an active Christian presence in the Fylde before 1066. The evidence is at best circumstantial, but it does seem to complement the record of a sixth-century crusade carried out by Bishop Kentigern of Glasgow from Cumbria to Wales, mostly along the coast. In contrast, the Domesday Survey of 1086 lists only three unnamed churches in the Fylde, though these are generally felt to have been those at Kirkham, Poulton-le-Fylde and St. Michael's-on-Wyre. Clearly the history of the pre-Norman church in the Fylde is shrouded in mystery.

The early settlers who colonised the Fylde have left their mark on the landscape in another way — in the basic shape of their communities. One of the most common forms of nucleated settlement in northern Europe is the street village, composed of a main street often running east-west, intersected at right-angles by another, shorter street; both would be lined by farmhouses and cottages, sometimes with a service road or back lane parallel to the main axis, and all set amid large open fields in which each inhabitant had some strips to farm. Although scholars have recently begun to question the concept of a fully-fledged and imported village structure from northern Europe with its familiar strip farming pattern, these basic street villages can be recognised in the modern landscape at Great Eccleston, Kirkham, Freckleton, and Newton-with-Scales in particular, though any open fields which may have existed have long since disappeared; those at Kirkham were enclosed between 1554 and 1556, and it seems likely that elsewhere enclosure had taken place as early as the thirteenth century. Of the other common form of settlement, the green village, which is so picturesque in North Yorkshire and county Durham, the Fylde has only one example, at Wrea Green, though it seems possible that the present Market Place in Poulton-le-Fylde may be a former green. The Fylde villages, particularly those based on the street plan, have remained fairly open until recent years when modern developments have produced infilling of the main street, but this feature is still evident at Inskip, Pilling and Treales.

In the long centuries between the Norman Conquest and the Agricultural Revolution which had begun in most parts c. 1750, the Fylde and its villages seem to have led a remote and fairly poor life. Perhaps the major change which took place in landscape was the revival of life in many villages. The Domesday Survey reveals that all the modern villages of the Fylde existed in 1086, though only thirteen of them were inhabited, the rest being laid waste, presumably as part of the punishment meted out by the conquering Normans to the uncooperative north of England. The re-peopling of these settlements is far from clear but the vast majority were making some contribution to the occasional national taxes levied in the fourteenth century, and it seems likely that a fairly rapid reoccupation would have taken place during the twelfth century. It may well be possible to trace the revival of village life through the references to them in the records of the various monasteries which were either situated in the Fylde or held property there. In the area there were few foundations. At Lytham there was a Benedictine priory of the abbey of Durham and Cistercian granges, or monastic farms at Staining, near Poulton-le-Fylde and at Staynall near Stalmine; strictly speaking the Praemonstratention house at Cockersands is outside the Fylde. All of these foundations owned land in the Fylde, as did the abbey of Dieulacres in Staffordshire to which parts of the townships of Bispham and some of the hamlet at Rossall belonged. Compared to the large estates of the great monasteries, such as Fountains and Furness, those in the Fylde were quite small, and much of the land had found its way into lay hands even before the Reformation. Among the prominent ancient families in the Fylde, some of whom benefitted by the sale of monastic lands in the century after the dissolution of the monasteries, were the Cliftons of Clifton, who obtained former monastic property in Lytham at the beginning of the seventeenth century, the Westbys of Mowbreck and the Butlers of Kirkland. The majority of landed families, however, were rather small fry and considerable numbers were fined and dispossessed of their land for loyalty to the Roman church and the Cavalier cause during the sixteenth and seventeenth centuries. Widespread absentee landlordism does not appear to have been a feature of the Fylde, though mention must be made of the substantial tract of land in the central region, including Weeton, Treales, Roseacre and Wharles, and parts of Inskip, which belonged to the Stanleys, later Earls of Derby, for several centuries.

The remoteness which allowed the Fylde to become a stronghold of Catholicism after the Reformation also acted as a barrier to expansion and prosperity. The vast extent of ill-drained mossland ensured that much of the region remained unproductive, and agriculture was poor. Nowhere is this better indicated than in the lack of substantial farmhouses and halls built either in the period between 1580 and 1640 when much of England was experiencing a 'great rebuilding', or later when prosperity came to northern England. As late as 1795, a Board of Agriculture report criticised the lack of scientific farming and spoke of the 'exhausted lands of the Fylde', though the great rash of late-eighteenth-and early-nineteenth-century windmills suggests that there must have been some profitable agricultural activity. The result of this backwardness was a thinly-populated landscape with many of the villages being very small — in 1664 there were 30 houses in Hambleton, 40 in both Weeton and Newton-with-Scales, 42 in Great Eccleston and 59 in Pilling. Most of these would have been constructed of mud walls on a cobblestone base and roofed with thatch. The substantial house, normally of brick in this clay region, was more exceptional, but good examples can still be seen at Hambleton Hall Farm (102/381422) and Little Eccleston Hall (102/414398), whilst Kirkland Hall (102/480435) and Lytham Hall (102/355280), the homes of the Butler and Clifton families respectively, are the region's only big houses and date from the eighteenth century. From the end of the eighteenth century significant changes took place in the landscape of the rural Fylde, principally on account of developments in agricultural practices. The first major improvement to be carried out was the drainage of the mosslands, generally done under the stimulus of an enterprising landlord with sufficient capital to finance the work, such as the Cliftons and the Frances of Rawcliffe Hall who between them transformed the main mosses into rich cultivable land. The accompanying changes in the landscape in the south-west and northern Fylde must have been striking to contemporaries. The wide expanse of open mossland was replaced by a geometric pattern of large, rectangular fields, separated from each other by quickset hedges and drainage channels, crossed by dykes which are sometimes embanked, and all set in a landscape of dispersed farmsteads connected to each other by roads and paths of Roman straightness. A second aspect of agricultural change in the region involved new patterns of land use. Traditionally, the Fylde had been a grain area with oats as the principal crop, but the nineteenth century witnessed an important change in the relative proportions of land use; by c.1870 there was, for the first time, as much land under grass as under the plough and by the 1930s less than one-fifth was being cultivated. The great increase in stock necessitated changes in farm buildings, and these, together with the new buildings on the reclaimed mosslands, further transformed the landscape. The commonest type of new farm saw the house seperated from the barns, stables and shippons, all of which were grouped around a sizeable courtyard. Good examples can be seen all over Marton Moss, inland from Lytham, and north of the Wyre. An interesting combined example is at Little Eccleston Hall where the seventeenth-century house remains, accompanied by a quadrangle of nineteenth-century farm buildings across the road. The third major agricultural change was a response to the demands made by the urban centres of industrial Lancashire and the emergence of the tourist industry on the Fylde coast. The demand for fresh food led to the introduction of large-scale market gardening first on Marton Moss and in the townships to the north-west of Preston and later along the two arterial roads in the region, and also led to an upsurge in poultry farming which has dotted the landscape with glasshouses and wooden chicken huts.

These important economic developments resulted in significant rural depopulation in the central Fylde and the majority of villages either stagnated or declined because the new farming was less labour-intensive than the old. This characteristic was particularly marked in the second half of the century — Newton-with-Scales rose from 269 in 1801 to a peak of 381 in 1831, but by the end of the century had fallen back to 229; Elswick rose from 232 to 327 but declined to 227 during the same periods. Many other parishes only managed to retain their stability or gain marginal increases during the same hundred years — Singleton grew from 325 to 373, Greenhalgh-with-Thistleton from 374 to 404 and Upper Rawcliffe from 494 to 518. Economic factors were not the only influence on the fate of villages in nineteenth-century England; as ever in England, money was at the root of the problem. At this time, the funds for dealing with poverty were raised by a rate which was levied on property, and where villages were owned by one man, or a few people, the burden was very concentrated. Thus there was a tendency to control population expansion by excluding poor families from entering and persuading existing ones to leave the villages, usually by refusing to build new cottages and occasionally by deliberate demolition of houses. The effects of the attitude, though there is no evidence of harrassment, can be seen in Clifton-with-Salwick, owned exclusively by the Cliftons of Lytham, and in the villages on the Derby estate; in all of them, the population decreased in the nineteenth century. Not all villages were so unfortunate. If some experienced population control under the hand of a dominant landowner, others, where landownership was dispersed, acted as magnets to the more mobile sectors of society. As a result some Fylde villages grew into small centres of trading and general craftwork, and had a high incidence of paupers. Examples can be found at Great Eccleston with a 45% increase during the century, at Hambleton (37%) and at Woodplumpton (31%).

Although primarily an agricultural region, there was a small amount of industrial development in the nineteenth-century Fylde which inevitably changed the landscape. The principal activity was in textiles at Wesham and Freckleton, where cotton mills and sailcloth manufacture respectively introduced factories into the area. The former grew as a result of its proximity to Kirkham and to the Preston-Wyre Dock railway and experienced a remarkable expansion of 974% in the second half of the century. In Freckleton, the spurt came in the first half of the century with an increase of 72%. Also in the industrial sphere, a short-lived boom in salt extraction at Preesall led to a rapid growth at the end of the century when the population expanded by 59% in the final decade, but the promise was not fulfilled.

To the west of the main north-south routeway in Britain, the Fylde's remoteness was instrumental in retarding the development of a modern transport network, and in the late eighteenth century, tourists visiting the new bathing resort at Blackpool risked being lost in the narrow and often muddy lanes of the area. The national development of improving roads by turnpiking had only a marginal effect on the district with one small stretch in the south-east of the region, and the canal era also largely bypassed the district, though the Preston-Lancaster canal, in its attempts to follow the contour level and thus avoid having to construct locks, did meander into the eastern townships. It was the railway age which brought the Fylde into easy communication with the rest of Britain. The first railway, from Preston to Wyre Dock, was opened in 1840 to serve the new town of Fleetwood, but this soon led to the construction of branch lines to Lytham from Kirkham and to Blackpool from Poulton-le-Fylde, both in 1846. The network of lines serving the tourist resorts was completed with the 1862 connection of Lytham with Blackpool and the construction of the excursion line from Kirkham to Marton; finally, in 1870 the Garstang to Pilling, and later to Knott End line was opened, principally to serve the Over Wyre farming community. Although a number of these lines are now closed, their impact on the landscape is still visible in the form of cuttings, embankments, road realignments, level crossings and stations.

The principal characteristic in the twentieth century has been the post-war development of some villages as dormitories for people whose work takes them to the Fylde coast or Preston. Although there are few villages which do not have at least one small modern estate, the tendency has been for those nearest to the west coast and the eastern margins to become enlarged first, with a later spread into the inner Fylde. Thus development has taken place in the 'sixties in Staining and at Broughton but has only reached further inland to places such as Elswick and Inskip in the 'seventies. In so far as the future can be seen, it seems likely that the recent decision to cut the projected Central Lancashire new town quite severly will only add to this recent trend.

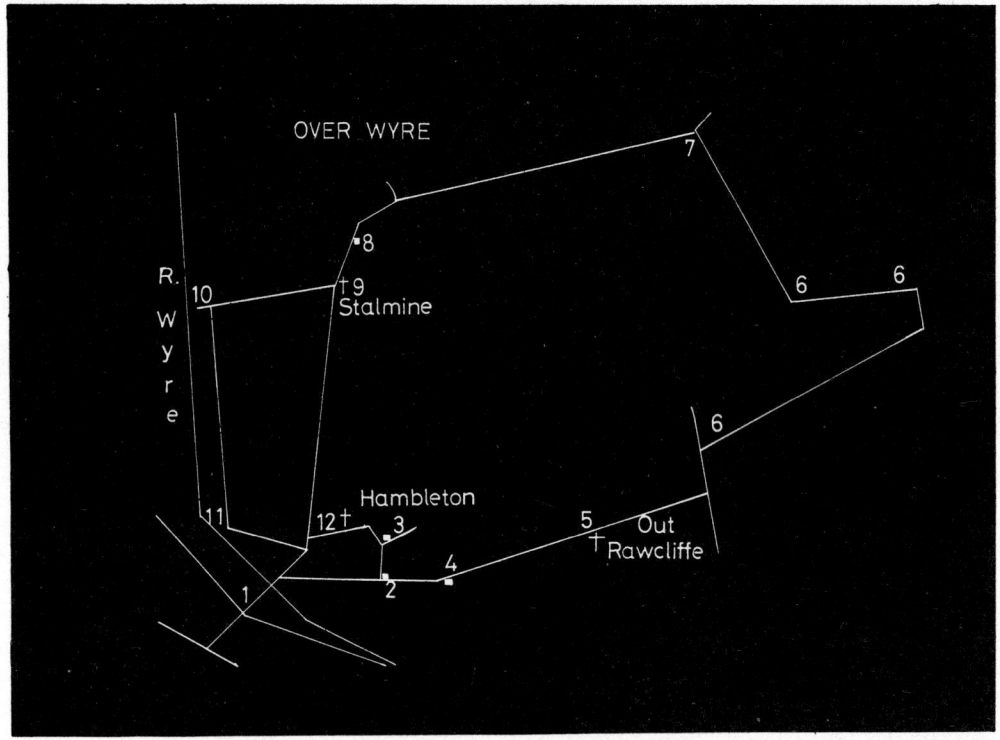

Fylde Villages — Excursion 1: Over Wyre

This excursion begins at Shard Bridge **(102/370410)** and covers some 20 miles. For detailed examination allow 2-2½ hours.

1. Shard Bridge: one of the two toll bridges over the river Wyre, and a glimpse of its origins can be seen on the toll board attached to the house on the western end of the bridge.

2. Mill Farm (381418): a late nineteenth-century four-square house faced in Accrington 'bloods', but note the remains of the old farmhouse with a former interior wall of cruck construction with mud walling clearly visible from the road.

3. Hambleton Hall Farm (381422): name suggests a localised importance. Dated 1710 with monograms IP, MP, RP, but almost certainly a rebuilding date — note the ledge along the E. gable suggesting some increase in height. A typical three-bay asymmetrical house with a through passage from front door. Close by, another but smaller farmhouse, now modernised.

4. Poole Farm (388415): inscribed 1756 RMJ. Rather more complicated house — a double-pile house in handmade brick laid in Flemish bond with stone quoins. Apparently the older type of three-bay with two central windows a large doorway until replaced by the 1879 porch to W. However, chimney stacks suggest otherwise. Rear cross wing of nineteenth century. In this general area, note the relatively small fields suggesting an old enclosed landscape.

5. St. John's Church, Out Rawcliffe (412424): a long way from anywhere, but central to the parish, a common feature in scattered rural areas. Brick and very plain with two rows of Norman windows. Interior has twentieth-century stained glass in E. window, a three-decker pulpit and an obtrusive organ. Were there three balconies originally?

6. Skitham Lane (426435): a general view of the newly-drained mossland indicated by (i) the roads raised by the removal of peat from the fields; (ii) differential field levels; (iii) farms on raised sites; (iv) farm names underline this — Primrose Hill, South Wood Hill, Black Hill, Island Farm: (v) the wide vistas over large rectangular fields bounded by hawthorn hedge and post-and-wire fences, all with their drainage channels: (vi) straight roads and tracks. All these features can be appreciated at any point along the road to Eagland Hill, also marked 6 on the map.

7. Head Dyke Lane (412478) offers a touch of industrial archaeology with the remains of the railway line and station at Pilling on the Garstang-Pilling-Knott End railway. This feature seems to have promoted the growth of an associated settlement.

8. Springfield House, Preesall (378467): dated 1758 TA, M, IB. Very late for this asymmetrical style even in the Fylde — another case of the datestone recording the rebuilding?

9. St. James' Church, Stalmine (375455): park by a good example of traditional Fylde walling i.e. a mixture of brick and a wide variety of stones. The church is 1806 and has a double bellcote. Side windows usually of two arched lights; no aisles and a short chancel. Interesting transfer of gravestone from yard to wall but the end product is visually unattractive. Gravestones contain some interesting warnings.

10. (355451): brine pumps in the fields to the north, remnants of the late-nineteenth-century salt extraction in Preesall. Beyond this point the road is protected from the Wyre flooding, and then rises up over one of the many drumlins in the area. Note how the scattered farms are sited on the E. and leeward slope of these gentle hills, thus gaining protection from the winds which have severly pruned the trees. Some sections of this road have high hedge-banks suggesting medieval field boundaries.

11. Down to Wardley's (365429): where hardly anything of the old port remains — see the staithe which went out to the ferry across to the now demolished Cockle Hall.

12. St. Mary's Church, Hambleton (379425): an early nineteenth-century church with a modern extension and tower to the west, replacing a tower of 1877. *Interior* — continuous nave and chancel with a shallow sanctuary. Large E. window with intersecting tracery and darkish glass, whose effect is counter-balanced by the six clear lights on either side of the nave. Modern abstract designs in new windows of W. wall. The substantial graveyard to the N. contains some good examples of nineteenth — and twentieth-century excesses.

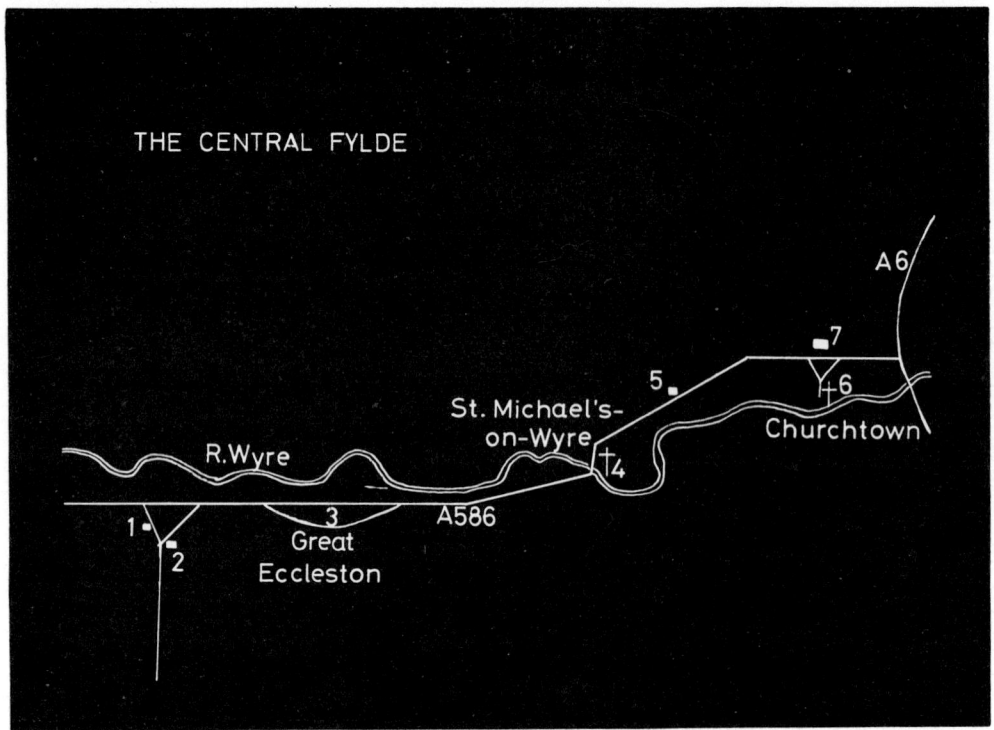

THE CENTRAL FYLDE

Fylde Villages – Excursion 2: The Central Fylde

This transect of the central Fylde follows the A586 road between Little Eccleston and Churchtown and can be examined in 1½ to 2 hours.

1. Wall Farm, Little Eccleston (412403): one of the districts oldest buildings with material dating from the sixteenth century. Note the mullioned windows on all sides, together with the substantial number of bricked-up windows on the south gable.

2. Little Eccleston Hall (414398) : two separate datestones on the rear of the house suggesting first a typical Fylde house (1638) to which a later wing was added on the west (1671). The overriding impression now is of a yeoman's house of the later seventeenth-century with one wing for services and the remainder for living. In the later seventeenth century, the house belonged to the France family who later became squires at Rawcliffe across the river. Over the road, note the splendid range of nineteenth-century farm buildings based on the quadrangular plan popular in that period. A few hundred yards to NE. see the barn whose exposed gable illustrates the structure and materials of the region's humbler dwellings of the time.

3. Great Eccleston village (430401) is set back from the river Wyre on a slight terrace, and in the High Street there is much to evoke its localised importance of earlier days; in the nineteenth century, three annual fairs were held, on 14 April, on the first Monday after Trinity Sunday, and on 4 November. The widening of the High Street to provide a market place is reminiscent of the traditional English street village. Worthy of note are (i) the range of housing on the N. side, from the Accrington red and rendered terrace

12

(1924) in the east, by the asymmetrical shop and barn (a former farm longhouse?), the later symmetrical facade of the White Bull and the adjacent cottages with their variety of roofing materials: (ii) S. side has Mulberry House, large and gabled with mullions, square-headed windows and oriels; next door a former thatched cottage with a projecting wing; further on the Black Bull with its four-square plan, sash windows and classical door casing, features common in this region 1780-1840; (iii) the E. end of the High Street has examples of renovation of traditional cottages — at corner of Chapel Street no. 79 Cobblestone Cottage (base of gable end) and no. 77 Mews Cottage — were these formerly one farmhouse?; (iv) the energetic can stroll into the village's Back Lane round the corner of Pax Cottage and return to the W. end of the High Street. Similar to Kirkham, this detour reveals something of the atmosphere of a rural village whose fields came very close to the main street and whose farmhouses were to be found in the centre of the community rather than out in the fields.

4. St. Michael's Church (462411): until the early eighteenth century, this was the parish church of the village of Great Eccleston, and may have owed its origin to the fact that this was, for centuries, the lowest crossing point of the river Wyre, an important fact when one remembers that it initially served townships to the north of the river also. *Church Exterior:* tower broad and low with diagonal butresses and crenellations which contain a date 1611 and the initials of Henry Butler of nearby Kirkland Hall. Both N & S. aisles embattled, the former with uncusped lights, the latter cusped with rather grotesque window stops. Tiny lancet window in W. wall of S. aisle suggests a smaller aisle originally. The whole of rather crude masonry though a slightly more refined E. end in sandstone. Beyond E. end, a vast array of polished marble gravestones of all colours, together with variously coloured chippings, but they do not spoil the visual appearance of the church.
Church Interior: everything low and dark, an impression encouraged by the dull, boarded roof of the chancel and the heavy Victorian glass of the E. window where even the lighter colours fail to admit much light. Some interesting fragments of fourteenth-century glass in the Butler chapel to the N. The wide arcades are late perpendicular i.e. sixteenth century; the clerestorey above is nineteenth and at this level there is evidence of an older roof.

5. Unsworth House Farm (466420): formerly Tithebarn Farm, this house may be important in dating the introduction of symmetrical styles into Fylde buildings. 1727 datestone presumably represents a rebuilding of an older house, probably a lower three-bay variety — see the ridge on the E. gable; in order to accomodate the theory, the first section of the barn to the end of the doorway would have been part of the original house.

6. St. Helen's Church, Churchtown (482428): formerly the parish church of Garstang though two miles from that town, it is often referred to as the cathedral of the Fylde, presumably because it is now the region's only medieval church.
Church Exterior: like its neighbour at St. Michael's, the masonry is crude, though it contains interesting features such as a two-storey Tudor vestry at the NE corner and an eighteenth century hearse house at the SW. The whole exterior is perpendicular with much crenellation and a tower (with stair capped by a little spire) and diagonal butresses. The re-roofing of 1811 has exposed the pitch of an older roof on E. wall of the tower. The motley collection of gravestones on the north side hardly add to the church's appearance.

Church Interior: evidence of a much older church than suggested by the exterior. Piers in the nave with Early English arcade c.1200-50, as is N. arcade in the chancel; S. aisle W. window is c.1300 as is the N. aisle W. window and the chancel arch. The blind entrance in the chancel suggests the existence of a chancel screen and loft at an earlier period. S. chapel perpendicular with a ceiling inscription of 1529, and the chancel roof appears to have been restored c. 1620. All the glass is Victorian, though that in the E. window is less dark than much of its time; the clerestorey dates from 1811 when the nave was raised.

Furnishings: the piscina in the sanctuary is c.1300 (see cusped heads) which suggests its original site may have been elsewhere. The choir has two rows of carved benches with rather inaccessible misericords of moderate interest. Pulpit dated 1646, though its Elizabethan decoration is testimony to the conservative character of the remote north-west (c.f. pulpit in St. Chad's, Poulton-le-Fylde). Oak chairs in the sanctuary seventeenth century; a classical screen in the S. chapel of same date; two-tier brass chandelier in the nave is eighteenth century, purchased with money subscribed to a restoration fund after a flood was erroneously thought to have undermined the S. wall in 1746.

7. **Churchtown village** contains little, but note (i) the vicarage to the E. of the church — a five-bay, two-storyed classical piece with a semi-circular porch and a shallow hipped roof; (ii) a pleasing five-bay house with a porch of fluted columns, hard by the church; (iii) market cross in the centre of the village, erected by Alexander Butler; (iv) Kirkland Hall **(480435)**, a private house of seven bays of two and a half storeys with a three-bay pediment. Facade dates from 1760, but rear wings are seventeenth century. Home of the Butler family.

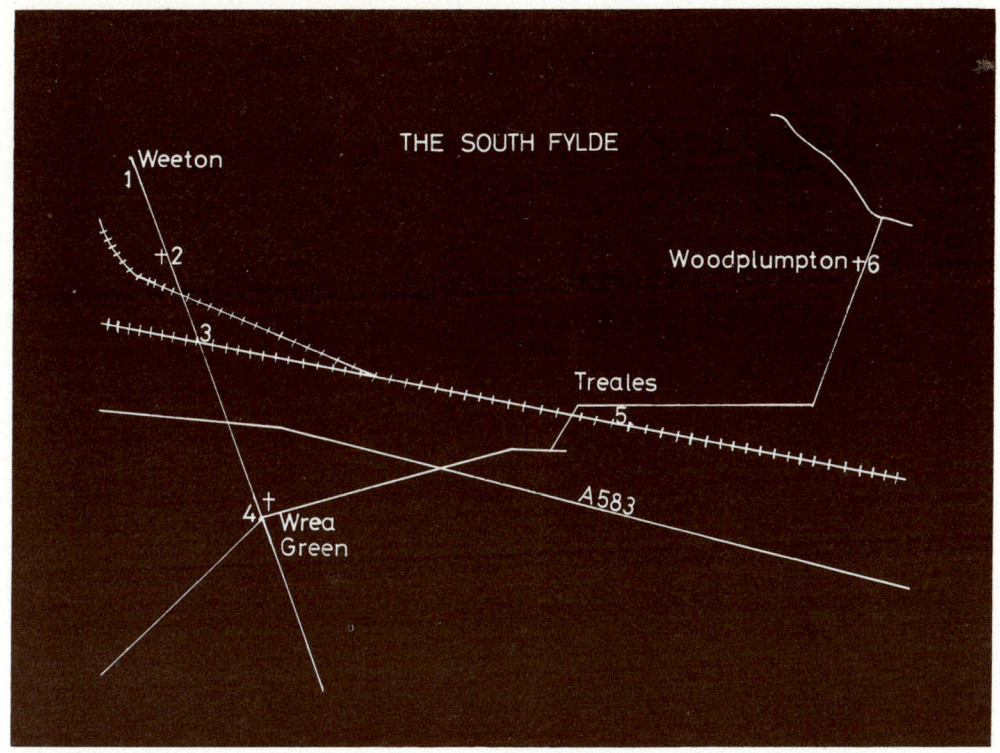

Fylde Villages — Excursion 3: The South Fylde

This transect is based on villages to the N. and S. of the A583 road and can be covered in 2 to 2½ hours.

1. Weeton (385346): a former estate village on the estates of the Earl of Derby, lords of the manor from the seventeenth century. Drastically altered and rebuilt during the 1960s and 1970s with only one older cottage recently rethatched, in the SE corner. Eagle and Child long established but much altered. Note how the property, on the sites of the old farm houses, clings to the main street (E-W alignment with fork at E. end), and how all the building is centred there — a reflection of the manner in which landlords controlled village development and population growth in the nineteenth century.

2. St. Michael's Church (385341): separated from the village, along with its school. An unprepossessing church in brick dated 1843 and 1852, with plain interior nave and chancel. Three lancets for E. window with rather dull stained glass; matching W. window. Typically incongruous gravestones to W. & N.

3. Shortly after passing over the present railway from Blackpool to Preston, note the land reclamation of the former direct line from Kirkham to Blackpool. To the W. it has completely disappeared, though a section has been used for the M55 motorway; to the E. demolition work is still in progress though only the cutting and embankment remain.

4. Wrea Green (395315): the Fylde's only green village, picturesque with its duckpond. Like Weeton there is considerable modern development around the centre but this village also contains a few well-hidden cul-de-sacs of recent property. Signs of its former character and economy can be seen: (i) the two farms whose buildings dominate the S. side of the green; (ii) two former thatched ranges on the E. side; (iii) the manor house, also on the E. side, though the earlier building is attached at the rear; (iv) the remains of a tower windmill along Mill Lane to the W.; (v) occasional houses in Ribby Road to the E. e.g. Hawthorn House and Rose Mary Cottage (a former longhouse?); (vi) Ribby Hall **(409318)** c. 1830, in classical style but not accessible to the public. The remainder of the village is a mixture of late nineteenth-century and early twentieth-century terraces and modern housing of a superior kind. St. Nicholas's Church:
Exterior: stonework rather crude and random, but dressed stone on the tower which has angle buttresses and a broach spire, all in the style of c.1300.
Interior: nave windows with trefoil and quatrefoil heads of c.1260; nave window has free-flowing tracery of early fourteenth century style. The heavy dark wagon roof offsets the advantage of light oak pews, and there is an uneasy juxtaposition of plainish panelling, ornate reredos and harlequin-tiled floor in the sanctuary.

5. Treales (442329): probably one of the oldest settlements in the Fylde, but its comparative remoteness has not saved it from redevelopment. This has included some modern building, though on a very small scale, but also some reconstruction of traditional cottages e.g. Primrose Hall Farm. The sparse development is, like Weeton, probably a function of landownership; the whole township belonged to the Derby family, a fact commemorated by the name of the village pub, an interesting building; from the W. a four-square house, but this is in fact an addition, at right-angles, to an earlier traditional three-bay thatched cottage with a S. elevation.

6. Through a landscape of compact fields and neat, though scattered farmhouses, some with dates (often noting a rebuilding), to Woodplumton, a large parish whose principal interest is in its church.
St. Anne's, Woodplumpton (499345): a Norman church on the site, but this building is early sixteenth century,mid eighteenth century and roofed about 1900.
Exterior: W. part of the N. wall has fragments of c. 1300 and includes a window with pointed-trefoil lights. The tower to the W. is capped by an octagonal lantern.
Interior: the north aisle was originally the whole church and is mid-sixteenth century — note its different roof. The present nave followed soon after, and the S. aisle is 1748 according to Pevsner; both arcades are perpendicular, though the one to the south is much cruder than its companion. The mounted bell at the W. end of 1596 and the Jacobean Holy Table in the SE. corner is dated 1635.

Old Mill Farm, Hambleton – remains of cruck frame and mud wall.

Hambleton Hall Farm 1710.

i

Little Eccleston Hall, a seventeenth century yeoman's house.

The Old Market Place, Great Eccleston.

St. Michael's Church, chiefly sixteenth century.

St. Helen's parish church, Churchtown — 11th to 16th centuries.

Market Cross and Royal Oak Hotel, Garstang.

Former Corn Mill on the river Wyre, Garstang.

Aqueduct carrying the Preston-Lancaster canal over the Wyre at Garstang.

St. Thomas's parish church, Garstang.

Market cross, stocks, fishstones and whipping post in Poulton-le-Fylde market place.

The Golden Ball, Poulton-le-Fylde – an eighteenth century coaching house.

St. Chad's parish church, Poulton-le-Fylde — eighteenth and nineteenth centuries with an earlier tower.

Junction of the old Preston-Wyre Dock Railway and the modern Preston-Blackpool line.

Skippool Creek and an old warehouse converted into domestic premises.

Hillside House, Kirkham — an early nineteenth-century town house.

Lower end of Preston Street, Kirkham.

Railway Hotel, 1840, by the Preston-Wyre Dock Railway at Kirkham.

Garstang

The small town of Garstang, situated at a crossing point of the river Wyre, occupies a significant position just to the west of the fault line between the Pennine gritstones to the east and the boulder clay to the west. These two factors have been instrumental in determining the origin, physical development and growth of the town.

The fact that any route from north to south had to cross the Wyre at some point, and that the river itself would provide an easy source of water were undoubtedly influential in establishing a settlement at Garstang. Known in the Domesday Book as Cherestanc, its etymological origins are thought to lie in a Scandanavian personal name, though this does not exclude settlement prior to the tenth century. In fact, it is possible to postulate the opposite. The parish church of Garstang is found, rather oddly, a mile and a half away at Kirkland, though a chapel of ease was established in the town during the later middle ages. It may be significant that the church of St. Helen, which dates from the twelfth century, is set in the midst of an oval churchyard, thought by some authorities to be indicative of a pagan religious site which was Christianised during the Dark Ages. If there is any foundation to this idea, it tends to support the theory of pagan and later Christian settlements at least within the parish if not the actual township of Garstang.

After the unhelpful Domesday Survey, Garstang had a succession of absentee landlords, amongst whom the Lancastres, barons of Kendal and Wyresdale, were prominent in the thirteenth century, and which later included the monarch who claimed the manor of Garstang in the mid-sixteenth and mid-eighteenth centuries. Its important position at the junction of the pastoral fells and the arable lowland, and midway between the centres of Lancaster and Preston, made Garstang an ideal site for a market centre, and indications of this function can be traced back to the early fourteenth century, though indications of an uninterrupted market since that time are less secure. The first incontrovertible evidence shows that, by a charter of incorporation of 1314, Edward II granted to the abbot of Cockersands Abbey the right to hold a market every Thursday and an annual fair lasting for two days on the feast of Saints Peter and Paul, 28 and 29 June. The fact that Elizabeth I confirmed and extended the grants on this charter in 1597 suggests that perhaps the original had fallen into some disuse after the dissolution of the monastery in 1539. The renewal coincided with very serious food shortages on a national scale following a series of bad harvests in the 1590s, and it is interesting to note that the charter speaks of 'the reliefe of the poore of the towne.' Topographical historians will also note that it was specifically decreed that the market and the two fairs, the one on the original feast day and the other on St. Martin's Day, were to be held in the 'streetwaie', a feature which has recently been revived. A final charter by which Garstang became a free borough ruled by a bailiff and seven burgesses, later a mayor and corporation, was granted by Charles II in 1680 when both fairs as well as the weekly market were confirmed.

This market function, in which the town acted as a focal point for a limited region, has been maintained to the present despite the advances which have been made in transportation which have tended to undermine the status of local market centres. In the last century a number of features underlined the service nature of the community. The present Market House dates from 1843, and the two cattle drovers living in the town in 1851 indicate the presence of fairs based chiefly on Scottish cattle being driven to the fattening pastures of lowland England. Any market town would have close relationships with its immediate area and be concerned to develop a mutual relationship. It is clearly significant that in Garstang in 1851, where the population was only 869, more than one quarter of the employed were engaged in a wide variety of craft work. The scale on which services in wood, metal, leather, building and clothing was provided pointed to a wider clientele than the township itself, and it seems likely that the servicing and market function of Garstang would be provided for at least the whole parish of 7,465 and maybe more. In addition, there were workers in Garstang who found their employment outside the immediate township, especially in the neighbouring textile mills, thus reflecting the beginnings of the town's modern dormitory function. There were no farms within the township in 1851, but there were forty-nine farm labourers and servants who presumably walked to their work daily in one of the neighbouring townships of the parish. Similarly, although without its own textile mill, Garstang was home for a dozen workers including spinners and weavers, combers and carders; no doubt these folk found work in the mills on the Bowland streams. A similar regional service must have been provided by the handful of professional people who offered education, spiritual guidance, legal and professional advice, medical and vetinary care and revenue collection for the government.

In the early modern period, Garstang was a very small place, even by modern standards. Before the censuses of the nineteenth century our evidence of population is rather variable, but sufficient is known to be able to make some estimates and to indicate the main trends. One of the clearest estimates is for 1664 when the population appears to have been c.215, and it can be assumed that, since in this part of the country the population remained fairly static for the last forty years of the seventeenth century, that this was the approximate position during that period. By the later eighteenth century, when many of the plagues which had caused devastation in the past had either disappeared or begun to be controlled, and when food shortages do not seem to have been as severe as in former times, the national population increased and that of Garstang followed. The burial registers of St. Helen's church give some interesting, though brief insights into the economy of the town during the later eighteenth century. During the years from 1780 to 1786, when the vicar recorded the occupations of those whom he buried, we find that the township sported a wide range of craft activities typical of a market centre, including the basic ones associated with clothes, footwear and building as well as the less common ones of gunsmith and currier. By 1801, there were 731 souls in Garstang and this increased to 839 by mid-century. However, that appears to have been the limit of growth since the subsequent forty years produced a reduction to 808. During a century when the national population was growing considerably, largely in parallel with industrial development, this loss, small though it was, must be attributed to population migration. In an age when economic opportunity was to be found chiefly in the industrial towns, people left the countryside in search of wider opportunities and greater stability.

The geological fault line, marked by the prominent scarp edge of the Bowland fells, forms the historic road which linked the two substantial market towns of early Lancashire at Lancaster and· Preston, and this routeway has had a national rather than a local importance over the centuries. In medieval and early modern times, it was a route which had considerable military importance, best seen in its use by the Scottish invaders during the Civil Wars and the later Jacobite incursions. Thus it was natural that when major technological advances were made in our transport system after 1750, they would concentrate on improving existing routes. The first stage of development of the north-south routeway through Lancashire was undertaken in a piecemeal fashion with the adoption of the Turnpike system in various localities. Under this, private bodies were established and charged, by Act of Parliament, with the improvement and maintenance of an agreed stretch of road; in return, they were allowed to charge a toll. One of the earliest turnpikes in the county was the one from Preston to Garstang, later extended to Lancaster, thus underlining the strategic importance of the township. In the colourful stagecoach era, a typical distance which a team of horses would cover before resting or being changed was some ten to twelve miles, and therefore Garstang became admirably situated point for a staging place between the two larger towns. Described by one visitor as 'a very poore town' in 1750, Garstang became an important intermediate staging post during the days of the stage coach, and it is claimed that Sir Walter Scott spent a night in one of its hostelries in 1828. The evidence of this important period is still visible in the substantial, if plain coaching inns which litter the main street of the town, and older residents may well remember the former toll gate on Lancaster Road. The importance of this element in the town's economy is suggested by the 1851 census returns which include ten innkeepers, one postillion and eight ostlers out of an employed population of 392.

However, by that time, serious and successful challenges had been mounted to the turn-pikes' domination of transport in Britain. The stimulus to further improvements came from the demands of an increasingly industrial economy which needed something quicker, cheaper and more reliable than a network of spasmodically improved roads. First canals, then railways emerged as competitors for the bulk cargoes of the new industrial economy, but such was the location of Garstang that no changes in the method of transport, other than by air, could completely ignore the town. The introduction of canals, which dates from the Bridgewater venture in south Lancashire in 1759, led to an intricate network which covered the whole country. In north Lancashire, it was proposed to build a canal from Kendal, south through Lancaster to Preston which could than be connected by raised tramway over the Ribble to the Leeds-Liverpool canal north of Wigan. At the heart of this scheme was the two-way traffic of Wigan coal to the northern factories and both raw cotton and finished products coming south. Thus, at the end of the eighteenth century a canal was cut from Preston to Lancaster, unique in that it was a contour canal and therefore without locks. The area around Garstang was particularly suitable for this because the geology and topography of the district ensured that it could still be built on a fairly straight line. It was natural that the town should take advantage of the new facility, and a basin with warehouses was constructed just to the west where the canal impinged on the community.

The final nineteenth-century transport development did not, however, make any serious impact on Garstang. The railway mania which struck Britain in the 1830s and 1840s rapidly replaced the canals as the major arteries of the country's commerce and mobility, though not without some serious conflicts between rival companies. The situation in north Lancashire is rather unusual in that the canal company tried to take over the new Preston-Lancaster railway in 1845, but it soon had to surrender, and, as with many disputes of this kind, the latter succeeded. The Preston to Lancaster railway naturally used the wide tract of level ground between these two towns, but it chose to by-pass Garstang, and the present line and station is a mile to the east of the town and appears to have very little impact on the life of the local community. However, this was not the end of railway development in the Fylde, and in 1870 Garstang Town station, a revealing name, was opened at the eastern end of a new branch line from the main north-south line to Pilling, and later to Knott End at the mouth of the river Wyre. This line was promoted chiefly by the farmers of the northern Fylde who were seeking better transport facilities to the markets of industrial south Lancashire. However, this branch line, a late venture to begin with, had a fairly limited life, and its last train ran in the early 1960s. Today the Garstang to Knott End railway is the subject of industrial archaeology, but, as such, is testimony to the nodality of this small town. In the twentieth century, the fundamental importance of this routeway has been emphasised once more with the construction of the M6 motorway, but since motorways seek to avoid urban areas as far as possible, this also passes to the east of the town and has had even less impact on the community.

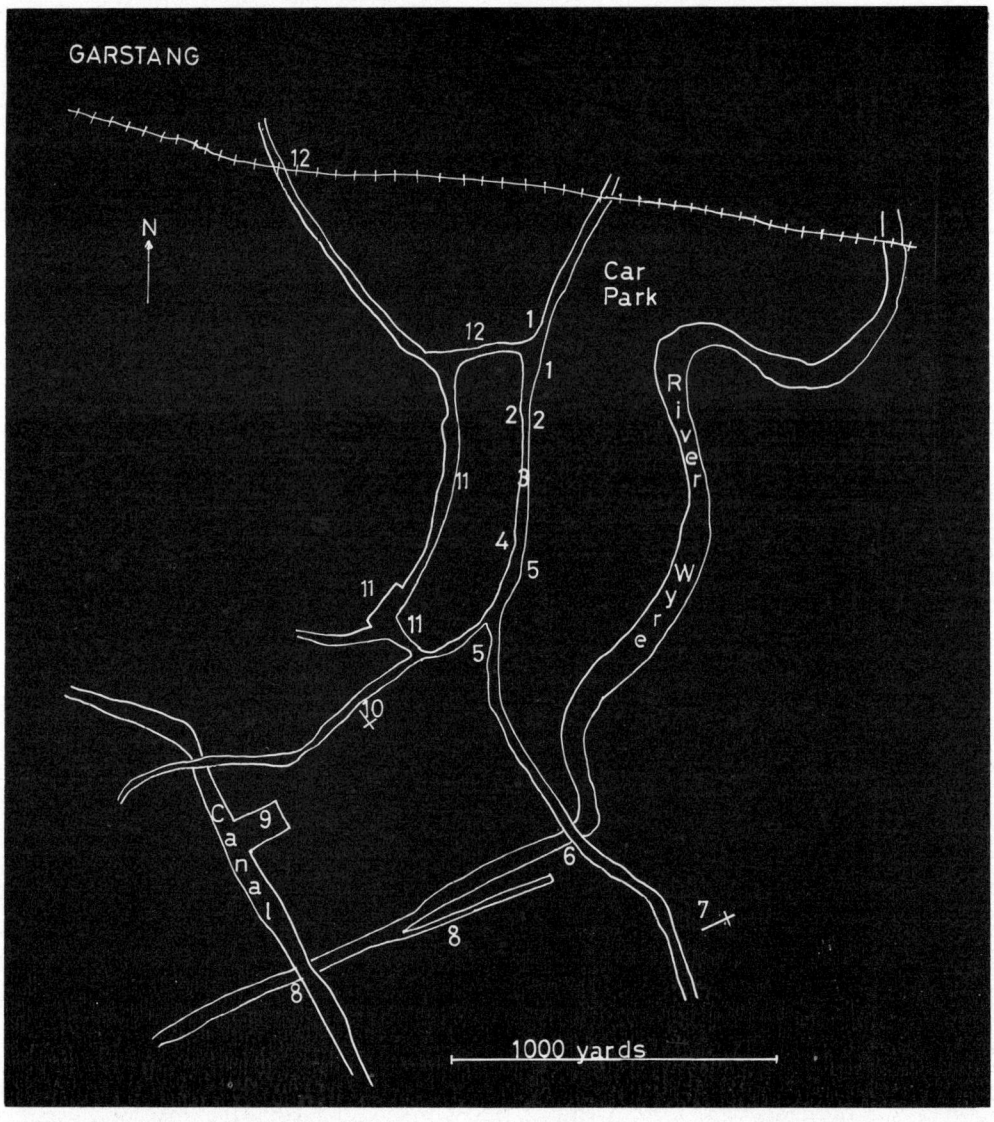

Garstang Excursion — a walk c. 1½ miles; allow c. 1½ – 2 hours. The shape of the village is a street which widens at one point to provide a market place and which is bounded by a back lane or service road, but Garstang is an exception locally in that its elongation is north-south with the river Wyre which has provided an effective barrier to settlement on the east. This orientation would also be influenced by the main routeway through the town.

1. Begin at the N. end of Market Street and notice (i) the old grammar school, a neat four-square building with rounded windows; (ii) Barnacre Terrace, a much restored, traditional stone cottage with rather heavy pointing — how many houses in this 'terrace' originally?

2. A brief stretch offering considerable visual contrasts; (i) on W. wide, the gable ends of No. 42 are of random rubblestone walling, common in the area from the sixteenth century; No. 43 has a datestone of 1744, but signs of blocked-up windows suggest that the symmetrical facade may have been different in earlier times; No. 46 is a rare use of brick (handmade) in a predominantly stone area, and its use of variable texture and stone round windows and doors help it to blend well with its immediate environment; (ii) on E. side, contrast the Crown Hotel and neighbour whose Accrington reds seem thoroughly out-of-place in this street.

3. A brief Victorian interlude with the brick Stoops Hall (1882) and the stone building opposite making use of various Gothic motifs — gables, quatrefoils on bargeboards; pointed windows.

4. Two good examples of the town's coaching days; the King's Arms, a neat, restrained building in coursed, dressed rubblestone with iron oxide stains producing an attractive facade; the Eagle and Child, a larger inn formerly an asymmetrical house (see roof line and chimney stacks), still with its coach entrance.

5. The heart of the market area: (i) the Town Hall, dated 1680 (Pevsner says 1755-64) and restored with original materials in 1939 — a brick building of three bays raised on a stone base of five courses, with stone quoins and window frames; central window with a pediment; topped by a balustrade and capped by a square cupola; (ii) next door to the N. the nineteenth century market hall; (iii) the Market Cross, a Tuscan column with a ball on top, was erected 1754 and restored 1897; (iv) the Royal Oak, a five-bay building of stucco over stone (see rear) — much altered and signs of an earlier house.

6. The eighteenth century bridge replaces a much earlier one. Below to the W. the remains of a fish trap and, less clear, of a weir which provided a head of water to power the wheel in the adjacent corn mill, now restored and converted to a house — the sluice control can still be seen, and the S. part of the building represents the unrestored nineteenth century corn mill.

7. Into the neighbouring parish of Bonds to St. Mary and St. Michael (R.C.), a Pugin church of 1857-58.

Church Exterior: a W. tower supported by buttresses with a stair turret; W. window in Decorated style as are louvres higher up; gargoyles near roof of tower. All windows have double-cusped lancets with a trefoil centre at their head — c. 1280 in style.

Church Interior: nave and N. aisle divided from each other by an arcade of six arches set on rounded piers with moulded capitals in c.1300 style. E. window also Decorated with typically dark Victorian glass, offset in the sanctuary by a dormer light. Reredos in high Decorated style with figures of the twelve apostles. Heavy timber roof of composite construction. Chancel and chapel arches have stiff-leafed capitals. Organ thoroughly unobtrusive in W. loft. Whole interior has a richness which contrasts with other local churches.

8. Return to corn mill, turn l. and walk through arch and by right-of-way alongside the river Wyre. Note the tail race, at the time of writing being filled in, by which the water was returned to the river; it enters the stream just before the aqueduct which is a small but dignified part of the Preston-Lancaster canal. Ascend the steps on the W. side of the aqueduct and walk N. along the towpath.

9. The canal basin for the town was once surrounded by warehouses, of which a few remain, in brick and stone, and the wider stretch through the bridge was a turning point for barges.

10. Leave the canal path and return towards the town centre to St. Thomas's Church, built in 1770 (nave) and 1876 (chancel) to replace an older chapel-of-ease which was under the jurisdiction of St. Helen's of Churchtown.
Church Exterior: very plain W. tower with obelisk pinnacles on top. Nave windows are Italianate and similar to St. Chad's, Poulton-le-Fylde. Size rather restricted which helps to account for the restrained churchyard.
Church Interior: typical late eighteenth century nave, constructed as a preaching house. The dark pews dissipate the advantage offered by the plain glass of the nave, giving a rather drab interior. Rear gallery on wrought-iron columns; roof based on cambered wooden beams. A very plain chancel whose unity is destroyed by the organ recess and whose floor has coloured tiles loved by Victorians. E. window of three Romanesque lights. Note the three Georgian houses opposite.

11. Proceed along Back Lane noting (i) the Wheatsheaf Hotel, an old longhouse whose S. section has been rebuilt in the Classical style; (ii) the Methodist chapel of 1818 in restrained Early English, though extremely plain and heavy inside; (iii) the modern supermarket development in brick, an unhappy but economic choice of building materials for a town on the edge of the fells.

12. The more energetic may walk along Park Hill Lane for c.¼ mile to the site of Garstang Town station, the E. end of the farmers' line across the North Fylde, though the remains are fast disappearing under modern engineering work; the more sedate will return to Market Street with a glance at the United Reform (formerly Congregational) buildings on the l, with the church of 1829, rest. 1886 (c.f. St. Thomas's nave windows), and the school of 1903.

Kirkham and Wesham

In a low and often marshy area such as the Fylde, it is inevitable that settlements will be found on dry-points, and one of the most obvious is the line of higher ground which is centred around a line from Bispham, through Kirkham to Woodplumpton. It is characterised by a series of discontinuous ridges and low hills, often steep-sided and separated from each other by hollows, and thought by some to represent the maximum extention of an ice-sheet during the later stages of glaciation in the British Isles, perhaps c.30,000 B.C. This natural settlement site was recognised by the Romans who established a station in the Carr Hill-Dowbridge area of the town and so vested the site with a localised importance which it has never lost. In medieval times, Kirkham was the centre of one of the large ecclesiastical parishes of the north of England, consisting of fifteen townships from the Ribble to the Wyre and including outliers at Goosnargh and Newsham. This last point is suggestive of the early economy of the Fylde, since the −arg or erg ending found in Goosnargh is derived from the Norse *sheiling,* a summer pasture; does this suggest some pastoral movement from Kirkham to the lower slopes of Bowland during the summer months after these settlements had been colonised by the Norse invaders of the tenth century? A second important historic function which Kirkham has enjoyed derives from its centrality in terms of communications. Just as the early site is emphasised by the Roman road which has been traced from Ribchester to a point a little west of Kirkham, so modern transport has tended to follow the same line of access into the Fylde. The combination of the above factors ensured that Kirkham would become a market centre, and any urban character associated with this was enhanced when the domestic textile trade was mechanised during the industrial revolution and the town became an important source of employment in the area.

Kirkham is a classic example of that most ubiquitous English form, the elongated street village oriented east-west along its morainic ridge, with a widening of the main street towards the centre to provide a site for the market, and with shorter roads leading away from the market place to the church to the north and the old town fields to the south. The evidence of placenames suggests that the whole area is largely one of Anglo-Saxon and Scandanavian in origin, though recent work in different parts of Britain indicates that there is much greater continuity of settlement from pre-Roman times than was once thought. The Roman fort, now obliterated by modern housing, indicates occupation before the Dark Ages, and the presence of a fort might suggest some local disaffection amongst existing peoples. The −ham in both Kirkham and Wesham point to seventh and eighth century Anglo-Saxon occupation of the site, and the prefix *Kirk*− suggests a Scandanavian take-over, probably in the early tenth century. However, despite the heathen, the name also indicates that the newcomers were either Christians on arrival or quickly evangelised, and it seems very likely that Kirkham was one of the three unnamed churches which the Domesday Book of 1086 records in the hunered of Amounderness.

In common with most medieval churches, St. Michael's, Kirkham, was associated with a monastic foundation; it was one of the three churches which Roger of Poitou, who obtained modern Lancashire at the Norman Conquest, gave to the abbey of St. Peter and St. Paul at Shrewsbury whence it was transferred by Edward I to the abbey of Vale Royal in Cheshire in the late thirteenth century. At the dissolution of the monasteries some two hundred and fifty years later, the living was constituted a vicarage, and the patronage of the living was vested in the dean and chapter of Christ Church, Oxford where it has remained to the present day. At the centre of a huge parish of almost forty thousand acres, the church of St. Michael must have experienced difficulty in serving all its parishioners adequately, and through the centuries a steady trickle of chapels were built, particularly in the more distant places, which by the nineteenth century had become daughter churches of the original, a relationship which is symbolised by their patronage resting in the hands of the vicar of Kirkham. Amongst the earliest chapelries to be created were Goosnargh (1330), Singleton (1361), Lund (1517) and Hambleton (1577): there followed in the eighteenth century Ribby-with-Wrea (1715) and Warton (1745); and the list is completed by Weeton and Wesham (both 1843) and Treales (1885). It is claimed that the origins of St. Michael's stretch back to c.684 A.D., a very early foundation in view of the fact that the north of England was only converted to Christianity in the seventh century, but the present building is of nineteenth century origin. The other denominations in the town date from the same period. The Roman Catholic church, designed by the elder Pugin, dates from 1845 and coincides with the considerable Irish immigration into the area; of typically uninspiring nonconformist Gothic are the United Reform (1896) and Christ's Church, Wesham (1843 and 1852), and Kirkham Methodist is an example of nineteenth century red brick with a modern addition.

Kirkham's market function can be traced to 1287 when Edward I granted the right to hold a weekly market and annual fair, and this function was formalised in 1296 by the grant of borough status by the abbot of Vale Royal. This latter charter, which gave the town a council of twelve and two bailiffs elected by the burgesses, did not carry the right to elect members of Parliament. There were forty burgage holders and it was their property which provided the qualification to control the affairs of the town. These consisted of strips of property on both sides of the four main streets of the town, had a frontage of some thirty-five yards and a depth of sixty to seventy yards. In addition to these, each burgage man held an allotment of arable land in the town fields of about seven acres. In medieval times, Kirkham was a village similar to many in England with its farms and tofts in the heart of the community and its principal agricultural land in the large open town fields which lay to the south of the township, though it is thought that these may well have been enclosed as early as 1300, and its main grazing area on the town moor to the west which was enclosed in 1554. The pattern of these early enclosures can be traced on nineteenth century maps which can be seen in the Lancashire Record Office in Preston.

By the middle of the sixteenth century, Kirkham had reached a stage of development which was to continue, largely unchanged, until the early nineteenth. Surprisingly little is known about its history in these years, but some important developments can be discerned. It was, of course, a small place, with an estimated population of 350–400 in the middle of the seventeenth century for Kirkham and Wesham combined, but it experienced considerable growth in the century-and-a-half following to 1,777 in 1801; by 1901 this had risen to 5,519 with the majority of the increase concentrated in Wesham in the second half of the nineteenth century. Population statistics are the bare bones of economic developments, and it is in an explanation of these figures that we must seek the history of the community over the last three hundred years.

In the period before c.1700, Kirkham was a small market and ecclesiastical centre which enjoyed some importance locally based on these two functions, but whose potential for growth was restricted by a number of factors. In the pre-industrial economy, profitable farming is the basic requirement for progress, but there is little evidence of this in the

Fylde. Population was effectively controlled by the natural factors of disease and famine and there are numerous examples before 1700 when major visitations, such as the plague of 1631, and serious food shortages, such as that which occured as late as 1728-29, cut back the population quite drastically; evidence suggests that most communities took a decade to reach their pre-disaster figure. Against this background, farming was not likely to develop and prosper. Probate inventories of the later seventeenth century emphasise the primacy of farming within the community, but also reveal a tendency towards some specialisation in occupation — we meet tanners, blacksmiths, linen-websters and attorneys whose presence suggests that farming in Kirkham was far beyond the subsistence level. The same documents also offer some insight into housing which, though usually of timber frame with mud infilling and thatched roof, varied from the substantial burgage house of several bays to the more modest cottage with a living room, one or two chambers and a buttery and a loft, to the humblest dwellings consisting of one room perhaps with a loft.

Of increasing importance in the eighteenth century was the domestic flax trade carried on in Kirkham and district under the supervision of the principal merchant families of the town — the Langtons, Shepherds and, later, Birleys. These men, whose families began life as woollen drapers in the seventeenth century, were substantial flax merchants, importing raw material on a large scale from the Baltic through the port of Wardleys on the east of the river Wyre, close to Poulton-le-Fylde, and between them, they organised a domestic industry which provided employment for many handloom weavers. The trade's importance is indicated by surviving apprenticeship indentures for the eighteenth century which show that of two hundred and forty eight children, sixty-six were put to fax dressing, sixty to spinning or weaving, and forty-three to cordwaining. It was from this domestic base that the flax merchants, principally the Birleys, were able to transform Kirkham into a factory town in the nineteenth century and which undoubtedly was at the root of the major increase in population. The impact of this development on the town was twofold. Firstly, major changes occured in the local landscape. In addition to Birley's mill in Cloice Meadow, built in the eighteenth and enlarged in the nineteenth century, the manufacturers constructed impressive town houses for themselves and cottages for their employees, both in the Irish quarter around the west end of the town and in the cottages to the south of the main street. Secondly, these families made an impressive social impact on the town, forming a wealthy and closely-intermarried elite which dominated all aspects of the town's life. Not only did they provide most of the employ-ment in the town, either directly or indirectly; they also accepted their responsibilities as social leaders by re-organising the grammar school, endowing charities, serving as bailiffs and thirtymen, founding and maintaining a girls' school, rebuilding the parish church, chairing and dominating the Local Board of Health which was established in 1852, and providing county magistrates by 1851. This last distinction underlined the status and leadership which the Birleys had in Kirkham by the mid-nineteenth century, and represented public recognition of the town's dependance of a paternalistic oligarchy. It is not an exaggeration to claim that the prosperity of the flax merchants and the town were synonymous for over a century and a half.

The introduction of railways into the Fylde by Sir Peter Hesketh Fleetwood in 1840 was part of his venture at the mouth of the river Wyre and not intended to be of specific relevance to the needs or the economy of the remainder of the Fylde, but it was inevitable that the region should experience some benefits. Just as Kirkham's topography had determined both the site and plan of the early settlement, so it was to govern the line of the railway. Anxious to choose the easiest route across the Fylde, the engineers naturally avoided the Kirkham ridge and the railway passed the town about half a mile to the north of the main settlement, passing through the tiny hamlet of Wesham which, in 1840, was a few houses down a side lane near Mowbreck Hall. The immediate result was the creation of a railway community at Wesham which rapidly became a small industrial centre as manufacturers moved in to take advantage of the sites which were available by the railway. Today, the two communities of Kirkham and Wesham have been linked by ribbon development and the character of nineteenth century Wesham has been altered by successive road improvements, but it is still possible to recognise what was the new suburb of 1850.

The population of Kirkham reached its peak in 1891 and that of Wesham a decade later, so that the story of this community in the twentieth century has, until recent dormitory developments, been one of decline. The slow and painful contraction of the Lancashire cotton industry has brought stagnation or decline to many communities in the last fifty years, and not all have found immediate substitutes, particularly those which, like Kirkham and Wesham, are rather isolated from the mainstream of the nation's industrial life. Today, there are no textile mills operational and the majority of the buildings have been demolished. Apart from a few light industries, such as a biscuit factory, Kirkham has now reverted to its traditional function as a market centre, with the open air variety being held on Thursdays and a modern shopping centre underlining its localised status despite the alternatives of hypermarkets and the like in neighbouring towns. Indeed although the popular cry would suggest that the small trader is being quietly strangled by the giants, the redevelopment of shop fronts and market place in Kirkham seems to suggest that Goliath can be resisted. In contrast, the architectural battle has been lost. The redevelopment of the market place, though only a small feature in comparison to some schemes of its kind, is hardly calculated to enhance the visual appeal of the town, and the shops stand uneasily cheek-by-jowl with imposing late eighteenth century brick structures and humble cottages of traditional local materials. The remaining post-war development has been the advent of housing schemes, the largest on the site of the Roman camp, and the emergence of a new role for the town as a dormitory for people working in Preston and other parts of the region.

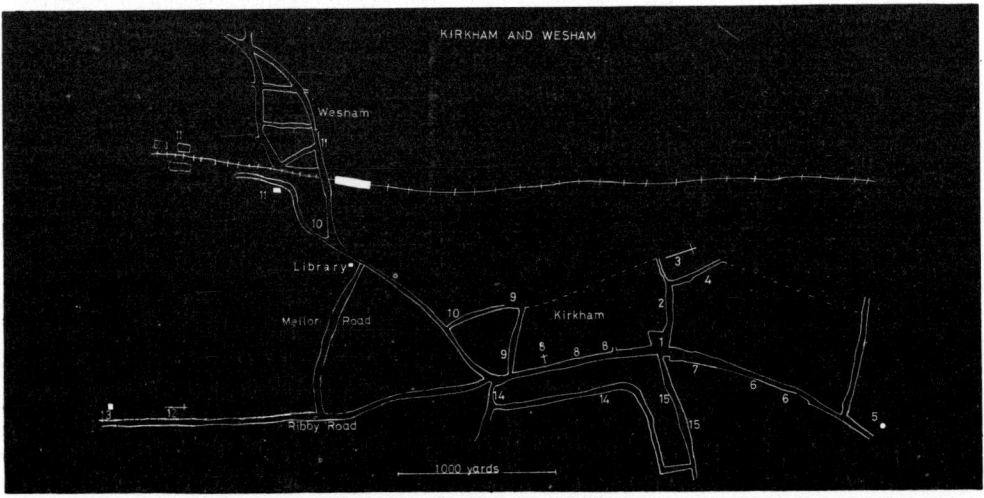

Kirkham and Wesham Excursion — a walk of c.3 miles; allow 2¼ hours.

1. The focal point of the town is the Market Place with its fish stones, and this is a good point from which to appreciate the plan of the town with its main street running east-west and the shorter roads to the north (to the church) and to the south (formerly the town fields). Was the main road once wider to accomodate the market? — note the encroachment of property on the corners of Freckleton Street. The Market Place has been the subject of modern development which has hardly added to the general appeal of the town — its use of grey-blue bricks and concrete is out of keeping with the rest of the town.

2. Church Street contains evidence of Kirkham's varied past; (i) Ash Tree House, now Church Memorial House, an eighteenth century building by the Langton family, replacing an older one on that site; a five-bay symmetrical facade in hand-made brick, laid in Flemish bond; central bay emphasised and there is a neat door casing in cement with a pediment and Ionic pillars; the whole edged with stone quoins and capped with a hipped roof; (ii) walk towards the church and note nos. 19-25 on W. side — formerly thatched and probably renovated traditional Fylde cottages; (ii) remainder of the street is unprepossessing nineteenth century.

3. St. Michael's Church situated, rather unusually, away from the main street but next to the glebe land which stretched N. to the present railway line. Rebuilt in 1822 at a cost of £5,000, raised by the church rate; steeple is 1843-44 and chancel 1853.
Exterior: a rectangular nave with tall thin lancets, common in this period; a splendid tower and excellent steeple — the former has set-back, stepped buttresses and is connected to its recessed steeple by flying butresses; crockets up the edges of the spire and gargoyles near head of the tower.
Interior: contrast the light airy nave with the rather gloomy chancel, the result of plain lights in the lancets and heavily coloured glass in the decorated-style E. window which is dedicated to A.L. Birley (d. 1871) — the effect is compounded by a dark reredos which runs the whole width of the E. end. The Nave has an attractive two-tier brass chandelier of 1725 and a Decorated tomb of the Clifton family in the S. wall. Rather obtrusive organ pipes illustrate a typical siting problem. Only the west gallery remains of the original three. Roof uses wrought-iron beams with quatrefoil tracery in the responds, and the crossings in this network are embellished with gilded foliage and the occasional grimacing face.

4. Across the road is the former National School of 1814, now extended, but the original of five bays with a three-bay pediment is clearly visible.

5. The early-nineteenth-century corn mill of four storeys, which marks the site of the old Roman station in Kirkham, has been heavily restored and converted into a house in the early 1970s. Formerly a brick tower mill.

6. Contrast the terraces of cottages built for the workers of Kirkham with the attractive Hillside House, home of the Birleys and built c. 1820-30. A fine town house of five bays in hand-made brick laid in Flemish bond; restrained classical doorway with a pleasing fanlight and iron railings on outer staircase. Across is the Black Horse Hotel with its classical, pedimented doorway.

7. Lower down Preston Street a series of cottages; nos. 30-32 older and assymetrical with covered thatch; no. 14 symmetrical, dated 1729 with initials H.I.E; no 10 which may represent a considerable rebuilding of a traditional house.

8. Poulton Street has an uneasy marriage of eighteenth-, nineteenth- and twentieth-century work all superimposed on the medieval street plan and burgage tofts. One of the few symmetrical houses is no. 34; the Gothic revival of the mid- and later-nineteenth century is represented by the Savings Bank (rather exaggerated) and by the United Reform Church (1896-97), a heavy and rather barren piece; the last phase can be seen in the Co-operative Society buildings of the turn of the century — here monotonous faced brick has been amended by the use of modern shopfronts on the ground floor.

9. Turn into Mill Street, the site of workers' cottages built in the nineteenth century and which housed the Irish immigrants. At the N. end was Birley's flax mill, recently demolished. The only reminders of the past found in street names.

10. At the end of Mill Street, turn L. along the interestingly named Barnfield, then r. into Station Road towards the nineteenth-century suburb of Wesham. Here, successive road improvement schemes have altered the landscape. The original road curved W. by the Derby Hotel and down the side of the present bridge to the railway.

11. The railway (1840) produced a new community centred on the Railway Hotel, a plain neo-classical piece, its adjacent cottages and the industrial sites (originally cotton mills) alongside the railway to the W. The railway bridge is late nineteenth century, presumably when road traffic was too busy to continue using the level crossing - see the datestones of terraces on Station Road to NW of the station.

12. Retrace steps to the library, turn r. into Mellor Road, to the end and r. into Ribby Road. Along to St. John the Evangelist and R.C. church by Pugin of the 1840s. *Exterior:* intensely cluttered graveyard detracts from the simple, even severe lines of the church. W. tower with broach spire i.e. pyramid-like sections connecting tower to spire. Louvres on tower with its set-back butresses on W. side; lucarnes on all sides. *Interior:* rather plain with arcade of six arches in Early Decorated style (c.1280) quatrefoil clerestorey does not admit much light, though Victorian glass in Decorated E. window is more translucent than many of its vintage; whole sanctuary well-lit by roof lights over the side chapels (c.f. St. Mary & St. Michael, Garstang). Organ in correct place i.e. W. loft.

13. Kirkham Grammar School, a building of 1909-11 by Greenway and Newberry, clearly influenced by the late-nineteenth-century revulsion against the formality of Gothic revival — Tudoresque with many gables and oriel window with transoms and mullions. Brick rendering over upper three-quarters.

14. Return along Ribby Road to West End, an evocative name. Turn r. into Orders Lane, reputed to be a corruption of Old Earths Lane, the path which led to the medieval town fields of Kirkham. Turn immediately into Marsden Street and walk along the old back lane — nothing of merit in the buildings, but of general interest to follow the old street plan of the community. Follow the road round into Freckleton Street.

15. Turn l. and return to the Market Place, noting on your way (i) the remaining nineteenth-century workers' cottages; (ii) the quaintly named hotel 'The Postman' — the 1851 census records show that a postmaster kept a public house in Freckleton Street; (iii) the new police station, another essay in concrete, a building material quite foreign to a boulder clay region such as the Fylde.

Poulton-le-Fylde

Writing in 1837, W. Thornber, the local historian of the western Fylde, described Poulton as the 'metropolis of the Fylde' and, although no one would claim that title for the town today, there is sufficient evidence in the contemporary landscape to remind one of its importance in the past. Situated on a low hill of glacial deposits which was drier and more fertile than the surrounding marshy area, and close to the river Wyre, Poulton-le-Fylde traces its origins back at least to the early seventh century and the Anglian penetration of the region, and it soon became the focus of life in this remote district. Historically, its pre-eminence in the area is founded upon its importance as an ecclesiastical centre, its port and its market function.

With the missions of the great saints, Augustine, Columba, Aidan and numerous others commencing at the end of the sixth and the beginning of the seventh centuries, Britain gradually became a Christian land, and the community was divided into ecclesiastical parishes to facilitate the work of the church. Itself probably a break-away from the massive pre-Norman parish of Kirkham, Poulton-le-Fylde became the centre of a parish of almost sixteen thousand acres some time after the Norman Conquest; included within it were the townships of Carleton and Hardhorn, both part of the urban district of Poulton-le-Fylde until local government reorganisation in 1974, Thornton, and Marton, now a suburb of Blackpool. The choice of the village as the centre of the parish was probably indicated by the existence of a church at the end of the eleventh century, though its origins are far from clear. It seems likely that it was one of the three unnamed churches listed in the Domesday Survey of 1086, and documentary evidence confirms its existence only a decade later. The dedication of the church is to St. Chad, an Anglian saint, and it has been suggested that this might indicate the existence of a pre-Conquest church on the site, but there is no clear evidence to point to anything earlier than the later eleventh century. Up to the time of the Reformation in the sixteenth century, the church of St. Chad was closely associated with monastic foundations, first with the French abbey of Sees and its local representative the prior of Lancaster, and later with Syon abbey in Middlesex. In consequence, much of the township also belonged to the church until the Reformation, after which much of the land in England came into lay hands and provided the source of the wealth of many of the famous and aristocratic families of our land. However, Poulton-le-Fylde does not appear to have fallen into the lap of any single substantial landowner, although the Rigby family of Layton certainly possessed a sizeable amount. Consequently, by the mid-eighteenth century the township had become a community of small freeholders and a few substantial tenant farmers, all free from the social control which was often exercised over villages by English landowners. It was in these lordless villages that rural nonconformity seems to have taken root, and it is no surprise to find thriving nineteenth-century communities of both Roman Catholics and Dissenters in Poulton-le-Fylde. The whole of west Lancashire was a stronghold of the old faith and many in the Fylde suffered for their loyalty to Roman Catholicism; indeed, Rossall Hall, formerly in the parish of Poulton-le-Fylde but now part of a public school, was the home of Cardinal Allen, a famous recusant leader of the later sixteenth century. After being compelled for many generations to worship secretly and barred from all local and national government Catholicism gained legal, though not always social toleration in the early nineteenth century, and a church was built in Poulton-le-Fylde in 1813, with the present building dating from 1912. The Dissenters were represented in the town by the United Reform, formerly Congregational church, which began preaching in 1778 and built in 1809 with a restoration in 1886, and by the Wesleyan Methodist who began worshipping in a cottage in 1819, built a chapel in 1861, and moved to their present modern church in 1965.

The local ecclesiastical importance of Poulton-le-Fylde in medieval time would almost certainly have contributed to the development of its market function, though the fairs appear to have been held by prescription rather than by charter. During the eighteenth and nineteenth centuries fairs were held for cattle and cloth on 3 February, 13 April and 3 November, with a weekly corn market on Mondays. As late as 1847, the local press was reporting the establishment of a new fair at Poulton-le-Fylde, to be held on alternate Mondays, based largely on the supply of cattle from Irish dealers operating through the new port of Fleetwood. Exactly fifty years later the parish council debated moving the cattle fairs from Church Street, one of the narrowest thoroughfares in the township, to a place where they would be less of a hazard to 'vehicular traffic'. Eventually, the cattle fairs were moved to a new market behind the Golden Ball Hotel in Ball Street, though this area has recently been converted for the storage of cars rather than animals.

Though the market function would produce a good deal of activity, it must be remembered that, by modern standards, Poulton-le-Fylde was a small place. It is difficult to gauge the population accurately before the introduction of the decennial censuses in 1801, but we know that in 1664 there were only 51 houses, producing a population of 205-230. There must have been substantial growth in the township during the eighteenth century since the population had reached 769 by 1801, and during this period a traveller described it as 'a neat little town built of brick and subsisting by trade and tillage'. Doubtless, the brick houses replaced the traditional Fylde mud-walled cottages which were the commonest form of house in the Fylde in the sixteenth and seventeenth centuries and which can occasionally be found even today in the remoter parts of the area. The basic economy of the township, as noted by our eighteenth-century visitor is amply borne out by the parish registers of St. Chad's church. Market towns normally provide a range of services for their customers as well as the basic facility to trade, and the burial registers from 1715 to 1740 include a schoolmaster, an apothecary and a maltster, two shoemakers, two tailors and two customs officers as well as thirty-two yeomen and forty-two husbandmen; by the 1790s the deceased craftsmen included blacksmiths, bricklayers and paviers, together with a small group of textile workers, chiefly weavers and flax dressers engaged in domestic industry. In contrast to much of south Lancashire, the rural Fylde experienced population stagnation in the nineteenth century, and Poulton-le-Fylde actually suffered a minor decrease in the years from 1841 to 1851. One of the clues to this is to be found in the total absence of textile workers by mid-century, for Poulton-le-Fylde never became even a small industrial centre, largely because of its remoteness and lack of raw material, and by 1851 it was a typical rural market town with a population of 1152 totally dependent on trade and farming as it had been a century earlier. The small town was dominated by a wide variety of craftsmen and retailers, with the shopping centre confined entirely to the Market Place, was provided with a sufficiency of basic professional services, had a fair scattering of people of independent means who sought to advertise their social superiority by the employment of a small army of servants, was over-provided with eleven public houses and off-licences, and has ten farms and sixty-three agricultural labourers, though many of these must have travelled out to neighbouring townships for work. In 1851 Poulton-le-Fylde's ten farms provided work for only sixteen labourers and were scattered around the periphery of the township; modern expansion of the community has meant that all of these have finally disappeared under the builders' bulldozers.

Changes in the mode of communications over the centuries have left their impact on Poulton-le-Fylde. In the seventeenth and eighteenth centuries there was a thriving port on the banks of the river Wyre about a mile from the centre of the village, and the township's name, literally the *tun* on the pool, points to a much earlier port, though there are no records to prove the point. Strictly speaking, there were two separate harbours, one at Skippool and the other at Wardley's creek across the river at Hambleton, but it is convenient in this context to treat it as one port. Classed as a creek of the port of Chester, its traffic was sufficient to warrant a customs house in Poulton-le-Fylde which was active until the creation of the port of Fleetwood, whence the customs post moved in 1840. Records of the activity of the port are scanty and scattered, but there is sufficient to paint a picture of a general coastal trade with Liverpool, Lancaster and the south Cumbrian coast importing goods for the market and exporting the farm produce of the Fylde, and of an international trade, particularly with Baltic ports in timber and flax, the latter of use in the domestic flax trade centred on Kirkham. More recently, diaries have come to light which show that north Lancashire families were emigrating to the Americas as late as the 1830s. Generally though, the increasing size of ships and the competition of neighbouring ports such as Preston, Liverpool and Fleetwood sounded the death-knell of the port of Poulton-le-Fylde, and today the visitor is confronted with a riverscape dominated by the leisure industry, though the careful observer will find remains of an earlier maritime activity.

The first railway in the Fylde, that from Preston to Wyre Dock at Fleetwood, was opened in 1840 and naturally sought the easiest route which meant ignoring Poulton-le-Fylde. The railway skirted the township to the north-east, but a small station was built at the junction of Breck Road and Station Road and a small community quickly gathered round it. Its importance was enhanced by the construction of a branch line to Blackpool in 1846, thus ending a brief but lucrative traffic for coach proprietors from Poulton-le-Fylde to the coast. The development around the railway was, however, both slow and small and the village appears to have gained little from its first railway. The present station, a late Victorian piece, at the edge of the Breck Road shopping area, was built in the last decade of the nineteenth century after a fatal accident on the hair-raising curve to the north of the original station had led to a re-routing of the line. This led to the isolation of the 1840 station though the line was not closed for many years and the sidings were still in use after World War II, thus promoting the development of a small industrial estate by its side. For a few decades, Poulton-le-Fylde had the luxury not to say extravagance, of three stations, completed by the erection of a small halt on the curve which linked the Blackpool and Fleetwood lines on the north-west of the village; the basic construction can still be seen from the second railway bridge along Tithebarn Street, but both station and line have disappeared.

The age of the motor car has also provided Poulton-le-Fylde with a by-pass with the construction of the A586 into Blackpool between the wars which relieved the rather narrow streets of the centre from congestion. However, the boom in car ownership and the redevelopment of the village centre in recent years have provided the town with a new lease of life and a new set of traffic problems. Needless to say, the one-way traffic system introduced to cope with the problem has not met with universal approval; what can be said, however, is that the town-centre redevelopment, if not everyone's idea of an architectural gem, has revitalised the historic market function of Poulton-le-Fylde.

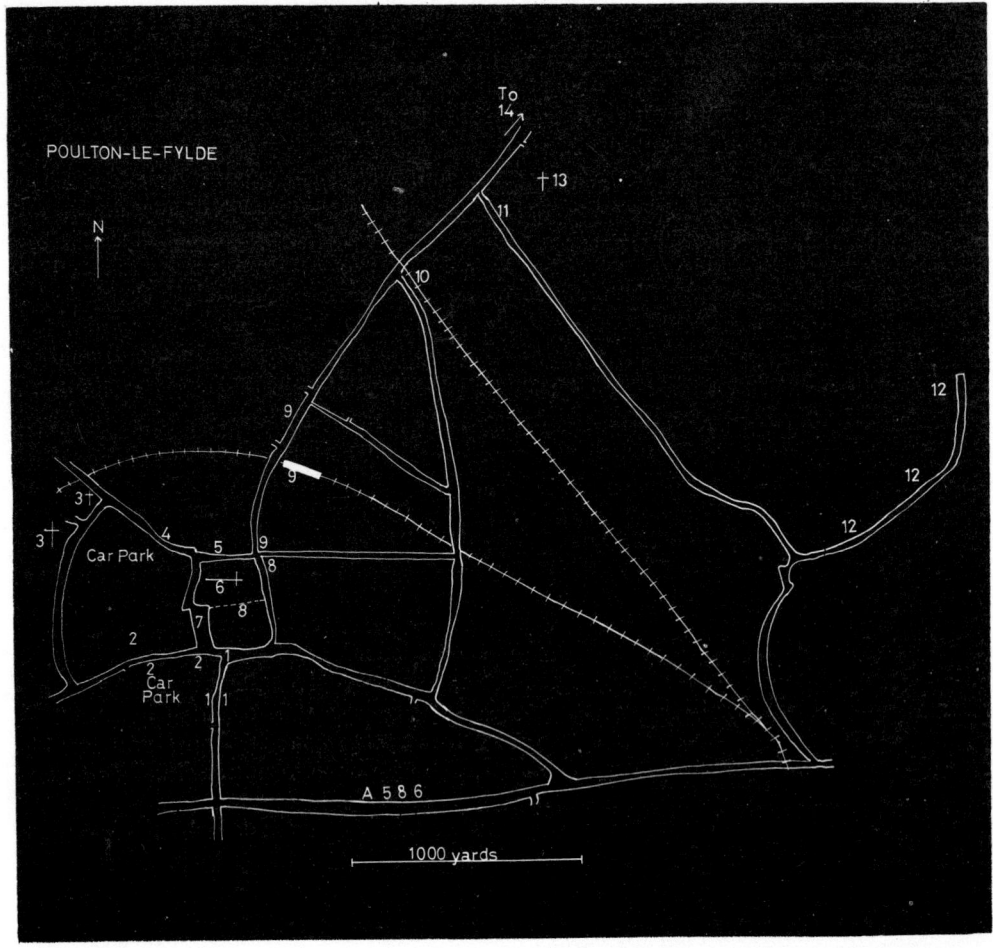

POULTON-LE-FYLDE

Poulton Excursion. (c. 1½ miles, allow 1½-2 hrs. including church visits)

1. Begin in Queen's Square; basically a nineteenth-century townscape, though the houses are considerably altered and there is some twentieth-century rebuilding. Modern development in rustic brick contrasts uneasily with the stucco and pebbledashing of earlier buildings. Note, on south side, a five-bay, three-storey house with two projecting wings, one of which has been rebuilt; classical doorway now recessed between modern shop fronts. A short detour into Hardhorn Road where Nos. 16,19 and 21 demonstrate the desire for symmetry prevalent in the late eighteenth and early nineteenth centuries, the former of hand-made brick distinguished by its irregular colouring and size, the later stuccoed.

2. Return to Queen's Square and turn w. across the end of the Market Place and into Blackpool Old Road, noting the classical house of hand-made brick laid in Flemish bond, also five-bayed and three-storeyed, of which about two-thirds remains. Almost the whole of the east end of Blackpool Old Road has been redeveloped since the war, though with little regard for the unity of the road; the rather dull south face of the new

Teanlowe shopping centre contrasts with the more pleasing library which received a Civic Trust design award in 1965, and on the north side there is a mixture of kinds and quality of brickwork.

3. Walk through the Teanlowe Centre, leaving NW to cross the carpark. Note the contrasts in modern developments on Queensway and visit the Methodist church, an angular building combining blue engineering brick and mineralite cladding. Opened in 1965, also with a Civic Trust design award, its overall proportions have been improved by an extension to the S. The whole inspired by the maritime connections of the township and of the Christain gospel — see the windows, lights and pulpit. Contrast the United Reform church next door with its Victorian Gothic motifs and Accrington red brick.

4. Turn R. into Tithebarn Street; only the name commemorates the tithe barn and the whole is now another dubious advertisement for redevelopment.

5. Continue into Ball Street, formerly much narrower than today with houses alongside the church wall. Golden Ball Hotel — symmetrical late eighteenth-century facade with Regency wing. Beyond, a fine classical doorway and fanlight; the rest nineteenth-century houses converted to shops, plus a modern supermarket. On right, the Thatched House, an early twentieth-century mock Tudor building replacing an old thatched inn.

6. St. Chad's Church is an eighteenth and nineteenth-century rebuilding of a much earlier edifice, of which only the tower remains.
Exterior: three periods represented from W. to E. i.e. tower early seventeenth century; nave a typical preaching auditorium of 1752-53; chancel of 1868, a product of the nineteenth-century reversion to mystery in religion and emphasis on the eucharist. Note also the classical doorways on S. side of which the door to the Fleetwood family vault, the easternmost one, is dated 1699 and belongs either to an earlier building or elsewhere. Graveyard cleared in recent years (though not without criticism) and stones used in paths around the church — allows a much improved viewing of the exterior. Note also the eighteenth-century cross on S. side on a much older (Saxon?) base.
Interior: characteristic contrast between a light Georgian nave and a gloomy Victorian chancel. The three-sided gallery, containing some box-pews, is supported on Tuscan pillars and access is by an eighteenth-century staircase. A good Jacobean pulpit and an interesting screen at W. end of S. aisle dated 1636. Georgian chandelier.

7. Exit into Market Place, the centre of the old community. On immediate l. a Georgian house/shop; the rest unremarkable. S. end has a gas lamp erected to commemorate Queen Victoria's Jubilee and the centre a garden to mark Queen Elizabeth II's. The whipping post, fish stones, market cross (probably seventeenth century) and stocks provide an interesting reminder of the town's former activities.

8. Leave the Market Place by Chapel Court, in the last century Pott's Entry and the town's slum quarter. The Corn Mill coffee bar perpetuates, in its name, the town mill which was sited there. Turn l. into Chapel Street (so named because the Wesleyan chapel was at its S. end until 1964) note the Trustee Savings Bank 1839 high on the gable on your R. and cross into Breck Road.

9. Breck Road; the last century has seen a transformation from houses and craftsmen's shops to retail shops. Note Conservative Club (formerly Ship Hotel), an ugly amalgam of Norman, Gothic and Venetian styles and motifs. On to the station containing one of Britain's longest platforms; note the monograms on the porch corbels telling of railway history i.e. L.Y.R. & L.N.W.R. A good wrought-iron station roof with Gothic motifs. Beyond the station, an area of late-nineteenth-century Georgian villas, now largely flats or professional offices.

10. At the junction with Station Road view the site of the first station — still visible are one platform, one siding and the old station house. From here into Station Road, noting the industrial estate and former gasworks on the l, presumably sited to take advantage of the railway, and the houses left isolated by the raising of the road to carry traffic over the new railway of 1896. Turn R. into Vicarage Road and return to town centre.

By Car (c. 2 miles)
11. Drive down Breck Road to the junction with Moorland Road — a significant name in any community and probably the site of the town moor (nineteenth-century maps show large, rectangular fields in this area, suggesting recent enclosure).

12. Along Moorland Road to Little Poulton Lane on l. The site of an outlying hamlet of farms, now a combination of picturesque and superior dwellings. Note no. 14 a three-bay, brick rebuilding of an old farm house; no 20 Abbotside Cottage, a twentieth century restoration of another old farm which has curiously added stone mullioned windows from a Yorkshire farmhouse — very uncharacteristic of this brick region; No. 24 is an old longhouse and dated. Little Poulton Hall, at the end of the lane is now derelict but was once a fine example of a nineteenth-century farmhouse and outbuildings.

13. Return to the junction of Moorland Road and Breck Road, turn R. and visit St. John's R.C. church of 1912. The former church of 1813 is to the left of the present one which is in stone. Both exterior and interior are particularly unremarkable, being undistinguished either by its masonry or its woodwork.

14. Continue along Breck Road to Amounderness Way, cross island, take road to Thornton and turn immediately R. to Skippool Creek. Note the dwelling house, Tarn Hows, on l., formerly a four-storeyed warehouse built 1741-44, but reconstruction is so thorough, including the removal of two storeys, that the only external evidence is the first floor brickwork, now whitewashed.